J355.4
1-3

22.00

24p

08

Battlefields

Jennifer B. Gillis

Holgate Community Library
Holgate, Ohio 43527

Rourke
Publishing LLC
Vero Beach, Florida 32964

© 2008 Rourke Publishing LLC

All rights reserved. No part of this book may be reproduced or utilized in any form or by any means, electronic or mechanical including photocopying, recording, or by any information storage and retrieval system without permission in writing from the publisher.

www.rourkepublishing.com

PHOTO CREDITS: All photos © Lynn M. Stone

Editor: Robert Stengard-Olliges

Cover design by Michelle Moore.

imprint

TK

Library of Congress Cataloging-in-Publication Data

Gillis, Jennifer Blizin, 1950-
  Battlefields / Jennifer Gillis.
      p. cm. -- (Field trips)
  ISBN 978-1-60044-559-0
 1. Battlefields--United States--Juvenile literature.
 2. Historic sites--United States--Juvenile literature.
 3. National parks and reserves--United States--Juvenile literature.
 4. United States--History, Military--Juvenile literature.
 5. United States--History, Local--Juvenile literature. I. Title.
  E159.G526 2008
  355.4'773--dc22

                                    2007017256

Printed in the USA

CG/CG

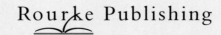

Rourke Publishing

www.rourkepublishing.com – rourke@rourkepublishing.com
Post Office Box 3328. Vero Beach. FL 32964

Table of Contents

The Battlefield

There are many places in the United States where wars were fought long ago. These places are called battlefields, and they have been preserved so that people can learn more about the history of our country. Some of the battles were during the Revolutionary War. Others were during the Civil War. There are also battlefields where U.S. soldiers fought Native Americans.

▲

An entrance sign alerts visitors to a protected battle site.

The Visitors' Center

The visitors' center is usually the starting place for a battlefield tour. You will probably see a movie about the battle that took place there. There are **exhibits** that explain what happened during the fight. Often there are displays of **artifacts** that were found on the battlefield. There may be **replicas** of soldiers' weapons and uniforms or flags.

This exhibit shows a scene from the Civil ▶ War Battle of Gettysburg (Pennsylvania).

Maps and Models

Models show just how everything looked at the time of the battle. Maps with arrows show how the soldiers moved around the battlefield. Small replica buildings, trees, and soldiers are placed the way they were during the battle. Models and maps show the whole battle as if you were looking down on it from above. Outside, you can only see parts of the battlefield.

▲ A model at Yorktown Battlefield shows
George Washington firing a cannon.

Holgate Community Library
Holgate, Ohio 43527

Who Will You Meet?

Many battlefields are **national parks**. Park rangers run the visitors' center and give talks about the battles that were fought. They may lead tours of the battlefield. At other battlefields, **interpreters** may give talks and lead tours. You may meet **reenactors**. For a few days each year, reenactors dress and live just as the soldiers did. They often pretend to fight the battle again so that visitors can see what it looked like.

Reenactors dressed as Confederate ▶ soldiers reenact a Civil War battle.

10

11

Walking the Battlefield

Your tour around the battlefield may be on a walkway. A battlefield might look like empty land or groups of grassy bumps and ditches. It's important to remember that the land was cleared and the ditches dug by soldiers trying to protect themselves. The walkways and boardwalks keep visitors from harming what may be left of a battlefield.

▲
A pathway leads past 18th century American
cannons at Yorktown Battlefield (Virginia).

Fortifications

At some battlefields you may still be able to see parts of **fortifications** that soldiers built, such as stone walls or rifle pits. Soldiers usually did not have time to build fortifications that would last a long time. Often, trees and dirt were their only building materials. Many battlefields have replicas that show visitors how soldiers used logs and brush to make fortifications.

▲
Sharpened logs were used as fortifications at
Petersburg National Battlefield (Virginia).

Earthworks

The best place to fight was on a hilltop. It was easier to watch what the enemy was doing from a hill. If there were no hills, soldiers built **earthworks**. At some battlefields, you can see miles of ditches and hills built by soldiers. They used logs to hold the dirt in place. The soldiers could fire their weapons from spaces in the dirt hills and hide in the ditches.

A cannon stands behind earthworks with log support ▶ at Petersburg National Battlefield (Virginia).

Weapons

In the Revolutionary and Civil Wars, most soldiers fought with muskets or rifles. Soldiers who rode horses carried long swords and pistols. There were also cannons that fired iron balls. Weapons were made from wood and metal, so they would not last long if they were left outside. Today, weapons like these are kept in museums and in exhibits at visitors' centers. Some battlefields have replicas of cannons outside for visitors to see.

Confederate guns called "Napoleons" stand on Henry ▶ Hill at Manassas National Battlefield (Virginia).

Monuments

Many people who fought on the battlefield were buried nearby, and you may see rows and rows of gravestones. There may be large statues of heroes from the battle. The statues and graves are **monuments** to the people who died there. Take time to read the words on these monuments. They remind visitors that it takes courage to fight for your beliefs.

▲

More than 3,500 Union and Confederate soldiers died in the Battle of Shiloh, April 6-7, 1862. (Shiloh National Cemetery, Tennessee).

Battlefields to Visit

Fort Necessity National Battlefield (PA)
www.nps.gov/archive/fone/home.htm

Gettysburg National Military Park (PA)
www.nps.gov/gett/home/htm

Kings Mountain National Military Park (SC)
www.mps.gov.archive/kimo/home/htm

Little Bighorn Battlefield National Monument (MT)
www.mps.gov/libi/

Shiloh National Military Park (TN)
www.mps.gov/shil/

Wounded Knee Massacre Site (SD)
www.woundedkneemuseum.org

Yorktown Battlefield (VA)
www.nps.gov/yonb/

Glossary

artifact (AR te fact) — something left over from the past

earthworks (ERTH workz) — series of ditches and hills dug by soldiers during a battle

exhibit (eg ZIB it) — something put in a place where many people can see it

fortification (for tiff ik AY shun) — something built to keep people safe

interpreter (in TURP reh tur) — person who explains something at a historic site

monument (MON you ment) — something put up to help people remember an important person or event

national park (NASH eh nel park) — land that has been set aside by a country for the use of all the people

reenactor (ree en AK ter) — person who dresses as people did long ago and takes part in presenting an event, such as a battle, that really happened in the past

replica (REPP lik uh) — something made to look just like an item from the past

Index

Further Reading

Brust, James. *Where Custer Fell: Portraits of the Little Bighorn Battle*. Univ. of Oklahoma Press, 2007.

Deford, Deborah. *The Civil War*. World Almanac Library, 2007.

Hess, Earl. *Wilson's Creek, Pea Ridge, and Prairie Grove: A Battlefield*. Bison Books, 2006.

Websites to Visit

www.cwbattlefields.com
www.civilwarhome.com/gettysbu.htm
www.nps.gov/apco/

About the Author

Jennifer B. Gillis is an author and editor of nonfiction books and poetry for children. A graduate of Gilford College in North Carolina, she has taught foreign language and social studies in North Carolina, Virginia, and Illinois.